YOU

Don't Want

A

Boaz

ROOSEVELT ETHRIDGE

Visit the author's website: WWW.RELIVEGLOBAL.ORG

First edition ISBN: 9781790419425

Printed in the United States of America

Dedication

This work is dedicated to women who have been abused, misled, and tortured by false love.

Contents

Chapter 1

INTRODUCTION

There are many women who are longing for a relationship and companionship. In addition to those desiring companionship they are discouraged with the hope of ever finding their special someone. Single women, whether they are single, divorced or widowed are told to wait on their Boaz. Many women are waiting for the guy that will sweep them off of their feet and provide for her in the manner of which Boaz provided for Ruth.

You don't want to be involved with anyone who turns your romance into a business deal or obligation. Boaz does not have to be in love with you in order to be with you. Boaz was a kinsman of Elimelech. Elimelech being the husband of Naomi was part of a group of men called the, "kinsman redeemers."

The Kinsman Redeemers are like a modern day fraternity or lodge.

They sojourned into Moab because there was a famine in Bethlehem. While in this place, Naomi lost her husband and her sons. During this transition, her daughter-in-law Ruth chooses to remain with Naomi while her sister remains home. Ruth made a commitment to Naomi knowing that she forfeits her opportunity for marriage. There are moments in a woman's life where she lives against the biological clock that ticks on the inside of her.

Ruth makes a decision to deny her biological clock. Even though the scripture does not give her age, Naomi acknowledges that Ruth along with her sister were still youthful enough for marriage. This is a striking proposal because remarriage was not promoted by widows. There are many women who suffer from loss. Traumatic experiences have the potential to shut women down and cause them to disregard the possibility of being found by love and/or embracing love.

Chapter 2
GLEANING WOMEN

All women possess a work ethic. Some women are more passionate about their career, home and talents more than others. Women are diversified by ethnicity and cultural backgrounds, however, you can find many great women in every community. Among these great women there are women who are awaiting the day to be acclaimed as someone's queen. Despite the length of the wait, the greatness of a woman is not diminished by time.

In the book of Ruth, "Ruth" is a woman who displays the greatness within womanhood. Ruth does not initiate a feminist position. Nor does she connect to Naomi with the intent to initiate women's rights. The connection that Ruth makes is with the intent to honor the life of Naomi. There are many women who have been connected to women who have impacted their lives in great ways. Ruth is an example of commitment. Ironically, Ruth gives an example of feminine kinsman relationship. Naomi was married to Elimelech who was a Kinsman Redeemer. Since, Ruth was a Moabite, she would not have known about the relationship of kinsman redeemers. However, with the death of her husband, she remained connected to Naomi without the desire of marriage.

Through this commitment, Ruth vowed to take care of Naomi. In our modern world, women are prone to having mentors and coaches. Many of these styles of relationships help the woman to become more proficient in the business world or provide self-help coaching for personal victories. However, there are many woman who desire companionship while being coached. There are some women who fall prey to internet dating or social media meandering. Many women find themselves trying to mirror the concept of gleaning in the book of Ruth in hopes of being noticed by a man.

There are some great qualities in the story of Ruth from her being noticed by Boaz. Many of the common observations have driven women to consider the gleaning stage as poetic romanticism. For hopeless women and anxious romantics, this scene would provide hope. Hope in the sense of being seen helpless but being committed would get the attention of the one who watching. There are many women who ask the same question, "where is Mr. Right." This question has many women challenged. Therefore, reading the book of Ruth has caused many women to end up with a "stay put" perception. This type of perception insinuates that a woman should remain consistent and visible doing mundane things in order to be noticed by men.

This theory has been adopted by many women that have sought or acquired companionship. Some would argue that it is the best way to be seen or get noticed. However, according to the text, romance has very little to do with Boaz's inquiry of Ruth. Women need more than inquiry in order to make an informed decision about a romantic connection. In essence,

Boaz inquired of the new person in the field. Once he was given her name and connection to Naomi, he quickly remembers his kinsman obligation. The reason a woman shouldn't desire a Boaz is because a true relationship is more than a business deal.

Boaz notices Ruth because of her newness to the field. Therefore, a woman can be attractive but beauty is not the security for love. Trust is necessary in order for love to be experienced. Also, building trust takes time and will never be established prematurely. You should never want anyone to love you out of obligation. Trust is not an emotion. However, trust can secure anxieties and silence some fears. The ultimate degree of love begins with loving oneself. Trust can always be destroyed when emotions and fear dominates a person. In the story, Ruth gets home from gleaning in the field and she recants her experience to Naomi about a man inquiring of her. Ruth's inquiry is one example of lacking trust in the one who inquired of her. Boaz is never required to understand your past, your pain, or your reality. Boaz's commitment to Naomi had to do with his commitment to the brotherhood. Would you really want someone in your life who could disconnect from the external in order to reach you internally? There are many women who settle for the shell of the man but never having the man.

Chapter 3
BUSINESS DEAL RELATIONSHIPS

Relationships are relational agreements that prove deep commitment's over time. All great relationships are tested. Infidelity is not the greatest test for relationships, but it is the most acclaimed and the most notable. There are many relationships that are picture perfect but lack ingredients that constitute a growing and developing relationship. Relationship is not a, "one size fit all", theory. However, there are many people who would like their companions and spouses to remain the same as when they first met. Many relationship experience failure within the first fifteen minutes because of the expectation of the person they meet to remain the same after they commit.

The "honeymoon" stage of any relationship does not compare to that quality of relationship developed over time. The nature of Ruth's interaction with Boaz was initiated by contractual terms. Relationships that are superficial are built upon contractual terms. Superficial in the sense that no one is required to love or be intimate as long as the image of companionship is visible. Image driven relationships can grant a lot of attention, however, they can decay over time. The reason for the decay is because human beings need more than pictures, outings and social events. There are many people who settle for the public fanfare of relationship while disregarding the emotional, psychological and physical needs of a companion. Ruth was not in love with Boaz. However, she was following the instructions of Naomi in securing Boaz attention. Naomi knew the responsibility of kinsman. Ruth would not have had the capacity to understand the nature of kinsman because she was a Moabite.

Therefore, you don't want a relationship with a man who fights more to impress your mother than he does to gain your heart. Business deal relationships will be encouraged by many outsiders. These outsiders can be your family, friends, co-workers, etc. These people are not prone to identifying how you feel as a woman, however, they would become more interested in the possible life-style change you will incur or public attention you will gain by this possible commitment. Economically and emotionally fatigued women are prone to finding the "business deal" option as refreshing. Business deals are great for business but horrible for romance.

Business deal relationships can cause you to live a dualistic life. Dualistic in the perspective that you could become focused on "outcomes and results only." In other words, you can find yourself becoming a "fix it" person for all of the issues and/or problems that occur within the relationship. Simultaneously, you can find yourself ignoring your feelings because the mutual outcomes are more important. Have you ever tried to keep a toxic relationship together only because

13

you were true to your verbal agreement while ignoring the shattering of your heart? Business deals can have the potential to overshadow a person and cause them to live the relationship out through their companion's emotions.

Business deals have leave you feeling guilty or emotionally responsible for the other person's condition. So, after Boaz found who Ruth was and her connection to Naomi, then he feels obligated to fight for her. You will cheat yourself if you choose to fall for obligated love rather than honest interest. Boaz is not concerned with your history as much as he is concerned with his obligation. For example, the person of interest should not be more focused having a relationship image that outsiders approve of and the relationship itself operates as a disregard to your existence. Economically battered women will find Boaz as a "knight in shining armor", until she realizes the knight is not there to protect her but there to protect the estate. Yes, the marriage commitment becomes the other person's property, however, many harbor disgust when they feel dishonored as property. Dishonor can come

14

through infidelity, lack of attention and/or lack of interest. When you embrace a business deal relationship, it does not have to make you the priority as long as the outcomes that were agreed upon are present and relevant. Boaz is not concerned with securing your life.

Chapter 4
WHAT TYPE OF MAN
IS HE?

Identifying the man is critical. There are many women who desire any type of man. It is easy to not consider what type of man is present in the relationship. A man can have great character, a wonderful physical appearance and great financial stability, however, that type of man doesn't work well with that style of woman. No woman should ignore the needs necessary within herself for a healthy relationship...."within" is key. It is common to accept external values as internal needs. However, a healthy and productive relationship needs more than external contributors. Focusing on external contributors can cause one to overlook internal values.

Therefore, knowing what type of man is present in the relationship is key.

Boaz is a type of guy who is proficient in business and economy. He is also a kinsman and is committed to brotherhood. This type of guy is not a bad guy, however, understanding what he brings to the table is key. The Boaz type of guy is driven by business and career goals. This type of guy is not the most vulnerable to emotional demands within the relationship. Within the story of Ruth, Boaz is obligated to the kinsman relationship. It is a great thing for men to have a commitment to brotherhood, however, relationships require attention to detail. Boaz has the ability to focus on the economic status of the relationship. If you are the type of woman that needs more than financial security and social wellness, Boaz is not a good fit for you.

There are many women who desire to connect with a "Man of God." This type of man can be wrapped in many different packages. It is most common for people to associate the term, "Man of God," with a man being priest, pastor or some form of visible leader. Along with this stigma, there are many of God's men who are overlooked because they don't fit the spiritual status quo. Therefore, there are other images of men that should be examined in association with the term, "man of God" in the modern day. It was most common in scripture for this term to be used in reference to a prophet. However, today, this term should be applied to a man's obedience and conviction towards God instead of his position or title in church.

There are men who fit the typology of Abraham. This type of man has purpose upon his life that unfolds overtime. The reward of being with this type of man is outstanding. However, walking with this man can present challenges and difficulties. Abram knew his relationship with God and the promise spoken over his life, but the process presented challenges. This type of guy can go through an identity crisis as well as extreme obedience. His notion to obey God can be costly as he works through his faith in order to be faithful to the word over his life. What will make this type of interest challenging is if one lacked the ability to comprehend his faith walk.

You could find yourself feeling second or not as a priority if the man is in the Abrahamic season of his life. The Abrahamic season of a man's life will lack explanation. Things will appear blurry and unclear and his clearance with God will be predicated upon his faith towards the father. Therefore, how should one walk in agreement with a man in this season. She first should be able to comprehend the difficulty of his obedience towards the father. Every initiative will not make sense but being the presence for him can build trust and security. Arguing about the call to obedience can become exhausting for the woman involved with an Abrahamic type man. One of the reasons for this type of exhaustion originates from the feeling of not being heard or received.

Just like any other man of faith, the Abrahamic man is built on covenant and loyalty. However, most of the time he will spend operating from a dual place in his heart and mind. This type of guy is about family and his heart to take care of everyone sometimes is his complex. Fulfilling purpose is important in the eyes of the Abrahamic type man.

The guy that has the typology of Adam is unique. This guy is not confused about his love or attraction. Almost upon first glance, this guy can identify and accept a woman as a wife. This type of guy is captivating. He is one who almost takes a woman's breath away. This guy does not have a problem with disconnecting from external people and giving the women position, place and a sense of need. This person has the potential to make a woman feel comfortable and ecstatic.

However, the engaging in a relationship unaware of the guy having Adam like characteristics can be upsetting. This type of guy can be needy or demanding as a result of his alienation of everyone and everything else. Loving this type of guy is great because of the space he gives the woman. However, the woman can find herself feeling incomplete or unfulfilled with this type of guy as well. The emptiness will begin with her desire of him to make and take initiative. It is not common for the Adam like guy to make many initiatives. This guy is good at his job or has a great skill sets. He is easily satisfied because his gratification comes from being with family.

The issue that occurs, is desiring the Adam guy to take initiative like the Abrahamic type guy. It is possible for the Adam type guy to be more traditional in his views. He could be more focused on gender roles and house hold responsibilities. He possibly could be challenged by who should make the most money or if women should work. In the time of trouble, Adam blamed the issue of failure on Eve. Therefore, this type of guy may be an initiator on many levels but moves slower in displaying security within the relationship.

A guy who is more like a Moses is community drive. This community is not restricted to politics or neighborhood efforts. However, this type of man is driven to the world beyond his home. It can become complicated being in a relationship with this guy. The complication would be in trying to identify his balance in prioritizing the relationship.

Many women with this type of guy can feel like she is sharing him with the world, this can make her feel like she is not important. Because of his call to community, he may feel it is important for him to serve the community in great ways. Therefore, knowing how to assist him in his ambitions and callings makes the difference. Making an argument about time and attention can become frustrating for both parties. Therefore, if a woman is interested in this type of man, in order to compliment him, she must be willing to embrace the call.

So, being honest and upfront is critical towards the longevity of the relationship. Many times women can be attracted to the guy and despise the commitment. This guy might appear extremely ambitious, however, always remember that he has fears. The Moses type can be outgoing as well as a social butterfly, however, he can be introverted and afraid of personal flaws becoming visible. Therefore, being with him is not to raise him as a parent raises a child, but the one would need to be able to coach him through moments of fear. Having this ability will cause the relationship to be closer between the two persons involved. The Moses type is not lacking desire of needing compassion. He just do not know how to turn off the call to community. It is not in the best interest of a Moses to try to cut off their call to community. Cutting off their call can cause them to walk around helpless and clueless to life.

Chapter 5
PURCHASED LOVE

No one wants to be bought for love. The idea of being purchased takes away the enjoyment of being free to love. A person can be bought with gifts, positions, and lies. I know being bought with lies sounds abrasive, however, many women bought the lie of a deceiver. There are many women who have fallen prey to a deceptive guy.

This guy was not into them because of love or affection. He did not cater to them because of their intellect or feminine strength. There are many who ended up with a guy that was their only to make his life better. So, the woman was manipulated by the theory of being submissive. However, it was never submission, it was a tactic for bondage or enslavement.

Boaz does not have to marry you because of love. In the story of Ruth, Boaz had a responsibility to remain Kinsman to Elimelech's family. Therefore, because Naomi was the living widow, the kinsman redeemers had to take care of their brethren's family. Yes, I know you are saying but she had a child by him Just because they had a child does not mean the child was born out of love. As kinsman redeemer, men were given the exception to have intercourse with the remaining women if no sons were born or alive.

You don't want to be with anyone who feels they are obligated to make you better. That it is a privilege that you are in their life. Boaz is about business. If you are interested in Boaz, he will count the cost of his investment of being with you most of the time. The bottom line for Boaz is that everyone wins.

Purchased love does not involve deep feelings. People walk around with surface emotions. These emotions are not discovered until years later in some cases. Love should not be purchased, it should be given. Being able to give love freely

25

and unconsciously is the goal to healthy relationships. Many people want to have the opportunity to loose themselves in the idea of love. However, if you are purchased, then your love is forced and demands an outcome that is usually favorable to the receiver only. Love is dualistic, it rewards the giver and receiver simultaneously when it is free.

Chapter 6
THE BENEFIT OF
BEING WON

Men are often challenged by the many desires and dreams of success that he may encounter. Men share in the same stresses of becoming a man. Common grounds of marriage, sexual orientation, worldly passions, family and business are all part of the common thread in men. However, it has become a greater norm for men to become weathered in trying to "stand" for God and not the "world."

Men who stand for God are categorized as *"God's Man."* These men have chosen to live their lives congruently with the word and character of God. *God's Men* are led by the Spirit of Christ. Also, these men walk in fear of God to produce his character in the earth. Ordinary (worldly) men are able to use their intuition to navigate life when pursuing dreams and goals. Moreover, there are good ordinary men who are not "Godly Men." Therefore, what define these men are their disciplines, perspectives, spirituality and their love.

Ordinary men will look within their resources to solve problems, establish business and care for a family. An ordinary man is not designed to understand spiritual things. However, a God's man depends on God as his primary source for thought, love and life. A God's man may not be well versed in scripture but he is devoted to walking in godly character. These men are more interested in their godly character more so than their social economic status.

A God's Man is needed, oftentimes he is overlooked and pushed to the back and classified unordinary. Society longs for good men, but the world will change when the *"God's Men"* stand up. These men will fight for justice, protect their homes, and defend their God. Recognizing and supporting *God's Men* will foster change in our communities, our homes and our churches. What's going wrong within our society is not only that men are out of place but it is relative that God's Men are not speaking. The best commitment a man can make is to become a "God's Man" and not remain an ordinary man.

When a man loves a woman, the love is authentic. There is no need for a man to be jealous of a woman's accomplishments who love him. However, the reality is, there are men who are challenged with inferiority complexes. They don't know how to embrace the growth of the woman they love. Therefore, sabotage and/or abandonment can become a reality of the relationship.

Men who are afraid of being out worked or shamed can be challenged with jealousy. Many times, men who are jealous can become overbearing and controlling. This type of domination can crush a weak woman and cause a strong woman to abort the relationship. There is no room for jealousy when trust comes through a process of learning each other over time.

Therefore, the spirit of intimidation is a silent killer within relationship. Intimidation is not a conversation that is commonly engaged by couples. It is common for people to associate time together as tenure that overrides intimidation by default. Because inadequacy is a real feeling, many men find it hard to walk beside a woman who does not possess the same inadequacy. This becomes a challenge for those men who see their inadequacy as a problem. Sometimes the woman has to suffer through his inferiority complexes. Her suffering is trying to not be confrontational about the inadequacy.

Women that love their man, inwardly do not want the outside world to notice the inadequate areas of the man. However, once a man notices these weak areas, he can run and hide in shame. Many women do not know how to respond to the man when he runs and hides. She can try various forms of communication as well as intimate environments, only to find herself blocked. Intimidation makes men run and hide, especially in times when he feels inferior. He can hide in his thoughts, his feelings, his dreams and his communication.

When a man is vulnerable in love. He should not compare his actions to the actions of his bride. Meaning, men and women both respond differently to life. However, it is not appropriate for the man to expect the lady to cognitively think through issues and life like a man. This is not stated to diminish the strength of a woman. Moreover, this is stated to acknowledge that some men use moments of decision and choice to reflect negatively on good women. Men have a tendency to lose the compassion that is necessary in hearing the woman out. Women need to be heard, communicated with and not talked down too.

It is not appropriate to compare the woman to other women. Even if the woman is the man's mother, comparing yourself to her is not the most ethical behavior. In order for the relationship to blossom into what fits for both parties, it will take time for each person to open up to learn the other person. It is hard to learn someone through the eyes of someone else. In this regard, men cannot afford to learn the woman through the comparison to another woman.

For example, Boaz could not learn Ruth through the lens of Naomi. Naomi understood this concept, this is why she coached Ruth on how to be present before him. Her coaching put her at the threshing floor and present in his space. Even with Boaz knowing who Ruth was connected too, he had to give space to learn Ruth for herself. Now, when dealing with Boaz, he is not obligated to learn you as a person as much as he may be interested in your gifts as a person. It is possible for Boaz to be infatuated with the woman of his choice and not in-love with her. So, the woman must make sure she is honest about her needs and her ability to give and expectations early on. Many women try to dummy proof their relationships by telling all of their pet peeves upfront, however, do not do that, give the relationship time to breathe and learn.

When the woman is won, the competitive nature of men is disarmed. Being won is not being lured. When a woman is lured, her value is not taken into consideration. But, when a woman is won, the total sum of who she is will be taken into consideration. In the book of Proverbs, the father teaches the son about the value of a woman. This woman is not classified by her sexual performance or her financial status. The quality of this woman is built around her character, personality, and

reciprocated interest.

Chapter 7
THREE DIMENSIONS TO A WOMAN

Every woman is made of three parts in her humanness. No different that man, the early philosopher Plato said that we are three part beings. He said, humans are: mind, body and soul. In the reality of being three part beings, women need communication and security in three dimensions. In the 21st Century, women need more than provision in house, car and income. You can have a woman that has the possessions but feel disconnected from the relationship because of not being reaching physically, emotionally and psychologically.

The topic about foreplay. A woman is not driven by intercourse as the sole fulfillment for relationship. Many would say that sex is good but in order to reach them physically that you have to reach them psychologically. There are many women who do not get to voice their sentiments of this desire upfront. However, this becomes bit of a cat and mouse game between men and women. Simply because men are deficient in communication. Men have a common nature of shunning effective communication. It is not because men do not desire to be effective communicators, the fact is that many men haven't been taught how to communicate his feelings more less his thoughts.

Therefore, relationships die because communication growth becomes an expectation of time being together. However, in order to reach a women physically, it will require a man understanding the dimensions in which she needs to be reached.

Reaching her emotionally is essential. There are times where a woman cannot explain where she is emotionally. This does not denote that she doesn't want to explain or converse. There are some women who needs the security of consistency and patience. Men are often ragged for saying too much or using the wrong voice inflations to communicate care, love and concern. When need to know that they are not classified as irrational for having certain emotional feelings. Embracing how the woman feels comes with being able to be silent, attentive and graceful in response.

Doing this will trigger a psychological response that produces calmness, love and care. If the woman ever feels as though she needs to me more assertive than normal in the relationship, she could lose respect and patience in the relationship. Women are nurturers but then need nurturing in relationship. It is not the responsibility of the man to become a "father figure" for his companion. Becoming a "father figure" in relationship can become a dogmatic position that disregards the value and presence of the woman.

Chapter 8
KNOW WHO YOU ARE

It is critical to know who you are before engaging in relationship. Relationship should not make you over but it should highlight the part of one's personality that is not readily visible. It takes time to learn who you are. In learning who you are, it will require embracing both of the 'good and bad' of life. The art of knowing who you are is detrimental to who you become vulnerable too in your commitment.

Vulnerability is not someone being blind to who they are or what they offer; neither is it an act of being silent without ever having an opinion. In the midst of choosing a mate, know who you are is critical in accepting what "fits." The fitting concept in association with relationship sounds like foreign news to many people. However, it is not foreign.

The "fitting concept" is a concept that suggest that two people are different but works well together. This is not two people have chemistry. There are people who have chemistry but are terrible couples. When someone "fits" into your life, they are not intimidated about the growth of the other person. Also, when a person fits, they are supportive of the other person's growth. When a person fits that will keep their individuality but try to find ways in which they are able to compliment the growth of the other person.

The growth is inward not outward. What people see outwardly should be the manifestation of what has been experienced inwardly. You cannot be a person who "fits" into someone else's life if you are driven by competition. Competing with that individual is not an ethical gesture in demonstrating love for that individual. In attempt to try to identify if the person "fits" or not, many Christian singles will attack the theory in Corinthians about being unequally yoked.

Unfortunately, in Corinthians, the scripture about being unequally yoked has nothing to do with romantic love. Over time, this scripture, 2 Corinthians 6:14 is talking about the mixing of faith between the people of Corinth and the new disciples of Christ. Many times Christians have used that verse because there was no other explanation for the separation, break-up or divorce.

When you are in a relationship, both parties will not be on the "same level." This does not mean they will not be compatible. The same level insinuates they will have the same drives, callings, interests, etc. This is not true, people evolve. The key to a successful relationship is allowing the person space and time to grow. Learning to be excited and receptive of the other persons growth is crucial in being a person that "fits."

Chapter 9
MAKING THE
DECISION

Being ready for relationship and being desperate are two different things. When a person is ready they can be excited by not anxious. Anxiousness can distort ones judgment. It can cause a person to overlook key things that are obvious non-negotiable items. However, the joy of being loved is enjoyable.

Love can create an adrenaline rush like someone getting a thrill from a roller coaster. Simultaneously, anxiousness can create an adrenaline rush as well. However, the cause of the relational high can be originated from a different when someone is anxious.

Anxiousness connects to the emotion of fear. When fear is present, it can impair one's judgment to make clear cut decisions. Love is a choice and it requires the clearness of mind and pureness of heart in order for one to be honest about their commitment. Fear can drive desperation.

Desperation is one of those things that cause people to feel as the only option for companionship is the one that is present before them. Men and women often want t know if there is more than one soul mate for them in the world. Actually, there is always more than one person in the world that can "fit" into the life of someone else. However, a person can only determine to romantically love one person at a time. If a person is desperate they can be irrational in their willingness to choose clearly.

Being healed and whole is key in having emotional clarity. A person can be healed and not whole. However, a person cannot be whole and not be healed. There are several types of healing that a person may need in recovering from relationship failure. Psychological healing is necessary. This type of

41

healing is when a person has been traumatically scarred and can't focus, think or retain information.

Emotional healing is equally important. This is the healing that transforms one's emotional stability. When a person has experienced loss, their emotions can be shattered. Shattered emotions can cause a person to be all over the place without stability. When a person lack emotional healing, they can be manipulated by guilt, gas lighting or narcissistic behaviors. Sometimes, in order to recover from relational failure, a person needs time alone. Time alone is a tool to access healing. A cluttered life only leaves to confusion or isolation.

Chapter 10
CONCLUSION

Women are indoctrinated into a thought into a culture of women who look for their Boaz. Many of who think that Boaz is coming to provide for them. There are some women who are tired of the chores and duties of maintaining living lifestyles as a single woman. The unwed women society is waiting for this many that will care for their lives as Boaz did for Ruth and Naomi.

You don't want a Boaz because you need someone to love you. It is not fair to you if you choose someone who does have any intentions of loving you inwardly. When you choose other men who carry various typologies of men in the bible, be mindful of what kind of man you choose. Men are not created in a cookie cutter way. All men are different. It is best to learn the man while he learns you in order to be honest with yourself.

Boaz is not a bad guy, however his model is business first and pleasure last. The Boaz complex are men who are driven men but disconnected. Boaz can grow to love you but he doesn't began with love at first sight.

55134198R00029

Made in the USA
Columbia, SC
15 April 2019